2/02

DEMCO

LONG
AGO
*and*
**TODAY**

A Farm Album

Peter and Connie Roop

Heinemann Library
Des Plaines, Illinois

Designed by Lindaanne Donohoe
Printed in Hong Kong

03 02 01 00 99
10 9 8 7 6 5 4 3 2

Library of Congress Cataloging-in-Publication Data
   Roop, Peter
   A farm album / Peter and Connie Roop.
      p.    cm. — (Long ago and today)
   Includes bibliographical references and index.
   Summary: Text, photographs, and illustrations identify and trace
patterns of change and continuity in American farms during the past
150 years, covering such topics as types of farms, farm buildings,
farm life, and the effects of weather on farming.
      ISBN 1-57572-601-7 (lib. bdg.)
    1. Family farms—United States—History—Juvenile literature.
2. Farm life-United States—History—Juvenile literature.
(1. Farms—History. 2. Farm life—History.) I. Roop, Connie.
II. Title. III. Series: Roop, Peter. Long ago and today.
S519.R75 1998
630'.973—dc21
                                                      98-18059
                                                        CIP
                                                        AC

Acknowledgments
The authors and publishers are grateful to the following for permission to reproduce
copyright photographs:
Cover photographs: Stock Montage, Inc., top; Phil Martin, bottom
Corbis-Bettmann, pp. 8, 10, 12,16; Stock Montage, Inc., pp. 4, 6, 14, 18, 20, 22 top, back cover
right; Steve Benbow, pp. 15, 17; Phil Martin, pp. 7, 9, 11, 13, 19, 21, 22 bottom, back cover right;
Grant Heilmann Photography/Linda Dufferena, p. 5.

Every effort has been made to contact copyright holders of any material reproduced in this
book. Any omissions will be rectified in subsequent printings if notice is given to the
publisher.

Some words are shown in bold, **like this.** You can find out what they mean by looking
in the glossary.

For David, Sue, Chase, and Clark. Thanks for your friendship and help!

# Contents

# Farm Life

*Children helped by feeding animals.*

A long time ago, most Americans lived on farms. Farm families worked hard. They cut firewood to cook their food and to burn to keep warm. They milked cows, fed animals, cleaned barns, cut hay, and carried water. They had no electricity. Few children went to school.

Today, few Americans live on farms. But farmers still work hard. They milk cows, feed animals, clean barns, and use tractors. Many farm families have someone who works on the farm, too. Most farms have electricity. Today, all farm children go to school or learn at home.

*Children still help on the farm by feeding animals.*

# The Farm

*Extra food and crops were brought into town by cart to sell at a market.*

Farms long ago were small. Most had less than 50 **acres** of land. But many people were needed to do the jobs on a farm. Farm families had many children. A farm family raised crops and animals to feed itself.

Today, farms are much bigger. Many farms have 500 acres of land or more. Some farms are run by one family. Other farms are so big, many farmers work on them. Farm families are not so large because machines do much of the work.

*Crops grown on farms like this one, feed people and animals across the United States and around the world.*

# Kinds of Farms

*Barnyards were alive with noisy animals and working farmers.*

Long ago, farm families raised many kinds of crops and animals. Cows gave milk, chickens laid eggs, and pigs were kept for meat. Farmers grew corn to feed cows and chickens. Potatoes, tomatoes, onions, carrots, herbs, beans, and squash were grown in vegetable gardens. Farm **orchards** had apples, cherries, or peaches.

Today, many farms raise just one crop or one kind of animal. Dairy farms have cows. Cattle farms raise beef cattle. Poultry farms raise chickens, ducks, and turkeys. Pigs are raised on pig farms. Orchards grow apples, oranges, pears, peaches, or grapefruits. Fish farms raise only fish.

*Dairy farms today often have hundreds of cows and use machines to milk them.*

# Farm Buildings

Farms long ago had only a few buildings. Families lived in a house or cabin. Animals were kept in small barns. Crops were stored in the barn, too. The house was heated by wood burned in a fireplace or a stove.

*Water was carried from a **well** or a stream.*

*Farmers keep picked crops in silos, like these three on the right.*

Today, farms have many buildings. The family lives in a house. Animals are kept in barns or special buildings. Machines are kept in garages or barns. Water is piped into the house from a well. Gas or electricity keeps the house warm.

# The Weather

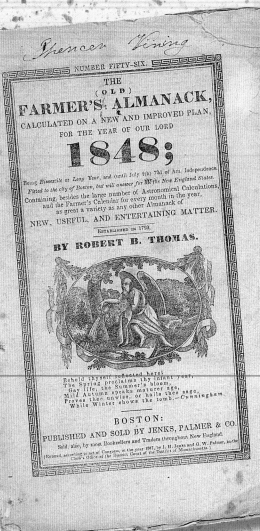

The Old Farmer's Almanac *from 1848 helped farmers predict the weather.*

Long ago, farmers closely watched the weather. Too much or too little rain meant a poor **harvest**. They watched the sky to help guess what weather they might have.

Today, farmers also keep track of the weather. Farmers listen to weather reports on television or the radio. Space satellites help them to better guess if the weather will be too hot, too cold, too wet, or too dry. Farmers still watch the sky to predict the weather.

*farmer watching satellite TV to find out the weather, 1998*

# Spring

*Long ago, plows were pulled by horses, mules, or oxen.*

Long ago, farmers plowed their fields in spring. Farmers planted new seeds for corn, wheat, and hay. They planted vegetable gardens. They took care of baby animals born in spring.

*Powerful tractors now do the work of many horse-drawn plows.*

Today, when spring comes, farm families plow and plant their fields. They use tractors to pull the plows. Vegetable gardens are planted. Baby animals are taken care of in warm barns.

# Summer

*Farmers cut hay with long knives called scythes.*

Long ago, farmers cut hay in summer. They tied the hay in bundles and stored them in a barn. The hay was winter food for animals. Some fruits and vegetables were **harvested.**

Today, farmers cut their hay in summer. The hay is used as food for farm animals in winter. Some early fruits and vegetables are harvested.

*Big machines chop the hay and pack it into bales. Some bales are square. Others are round.*

# Fall

Long ago, farmers **harvested** their crops in fall. Corn was cut and stored in bins and barns. Fruits and vegetables were picked and stored. Trees were cut for firewood. **Manure** was spread to make the soil better in the spring.

*apple picking, late 1800s*

*harvesting corn with a tractor and truck, 1998*

Today, farmers harvest their crops in fall. Corn, hay, and **soybeans** are stored in silos to feed the animals during winter. Fields are plowed again. Manure or **fertilizers** are spread to make the ground better in the spring.

# Winter

*Farmers repaired and made new tools during the winter months.*

Long ago, farmers rested in the winter. They took care of their animals. They planned which crops to plant in spring and where to plant them.

Today, farmers rest in the winter. They take care of their animals. They fix broken machines or have a **mechanic** fix them. They plan what crops to plant in the spring and in which fields to plant them.

*Farmers today spend a lot of time working in barns during winter.*

# Farms Long Ago and Today

Farms long ago and today are alike in some
ways but different in others. Long ago, farm work
was hard. Many of the jobs had to be done by
hand. Today, farm work is still hard. Farmers now
have machines to help them grow and **harvest**
the food we need.

# Glossary

**acres**  areas of land about the size of a soccer field

**fertilizers**  things added to soil to help plants grow

**harvest**  to pick and gather crops

**manure**  animal waste

**mechanic**  person who fixes broken machines

**orchards**  large groups of trees grown for their fruit

**predict**  guess

**soybeans**  kind of beans used to make oils, flour, and many other foods

**well**  deep hole in the ground where water is brought out

# More Books to Read

Brock, Claude, and Thomas Buss, editors. *Farming Once Upon a Time.* Louisville, Ky: Concord Publishers, 1996.

Kallen, Stuart. *The Farm.* Minneapolis, Minn: Abdo & Daughters, 1997.

O'Hara, Megan. *Pioneer Farm: A Farm on the Prairie in the 1880s.* Mankato, Minn: Capstone Press, 1998.

# Index